# staying dry

## last straw strategies

# last straw strategies
99 tips to bring you back from the end of your rope

# staying dry

## Michelle Kennedy

First edition for the United States, its territories and possessions, and Canada published in 2004 by BARRON'S EDUCATIONAL SERIES, INC. by arrangement with THE IVY PRESS LIMITED

All inquiries should be addressed to:
Barron's Educational Series, Inc.,
250 Wireless Boulevard
Hauppauge, New York 11788
www.barronseduc.com

International Standard Book Number
0-7641-2719-5

Library of Congress Catalog Card No.
2003107434

This book was conceived, designed, and produced by
THE IVY PRESS LIMITED
The Old Candlemakers
West Street, Lewes
East Sussex BN7 2NZ

Every effort has been taken to ensure that all information in this book is correct. This book is not intended to replace consultation with your doctor, surgeon, or other healthcare professional. The author and publisher disclaim any loss, injury, or damage incurred as a consequence, directly or indirectly, of the use and application of the contents of this book.

Creative Director PETER BRIDGEWATER
Publisher SOPHIE COLLINS
Editorial Director STEVE LUCK
Design Manager TONY SEDDON
Senior Project Editor REBECCA SARACENO
Designer JANE LANAWAY
Illustrator EMMA BROWNJOHN

Printed in China
9 8 7 6 5 4 3 2 1

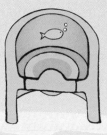

# contents

# staying dry
## introduction

Potty training can be a frustrating, yet ultimately rewarding, time in parents' and children's lives. It's the last big hurdle of toddlerhood and the one that strikes the most fear into parents. Don't worry, you will not mess up your child for life if you get off to a rocky start, but you can make things tougher than they need to be. Patience is the key to potty training and I'm not going to say that this quality of parenting is easy to maintain.

As with everything in parenting, there are many schools of thought about keeping kids dry. Many parents have discovered that it is easier to train a child to pee in the potty than to poop in it. Part of this, I think, is simply because one pees more times in a day. However, I firmly believe that potty training should cover both, right from the beginning. Allowing a child to do one and not the other will only create confusion and headaches later on.

And finally, whoever said that getting a child to go to a toilet made life easier was insane. For the first few months it can be sheer panic. It's much easier to clean out a contained diaper than to clean up the floor constantly (and the car seat and who knows how many pairs of pants). But it can be done and these tips will help you get off to a good start—and if you have already begun, they should help you get back on track.

# is your child
# ready?

You've been changing diapers for two, maybe three years, and frankly, you're sick of it. You're sick of the smell, the constant weight of a diaper bag on your shoulder, and the constant worry about whether or not there are enough diapers in the house. Maybe you have a new baby so you are doing double diaper duty. Wouldn't it just be easier if your toddler or preschooler was potty-trained? Well, maybe and maybe not. Potty training takes intense dedication. If your child isn't ready, then you're going to go nowhere, fast. And instead of easing your diaper load, you'll have diapers to change and floors and pants to clean. So, before you take this next leap, read these tips to determine if your child is really ready for that next big step.

# clean away

A sudden desire to be clean and to clean things is one indication that your child is ready to potty train. There will come a day (I know, you don't believe me now) when your child will want his hands washed. Or she'll want to disinfect the house with a baby wipe. Or maybe she'll come right out and tell you that her "diapers smell icky." This is good. Let her clean away. Have her help clean the bathroom

with that baby wipe and then you can say, "Oh, and by the way, have you met the toilet?"

# imitation is the finest form of flattery

2-4 years

I remember watching my third child take a book off the shelf, sit on a stool in the living room, and read. When I asked him what he was up to, he said, "Going potty." If you find your child imitating toilet behavior with a doll or by himself, this could be a good sign. This same child also had a habit of walking into the bathroom while I was in there. After shooing him out the first few times, it occurred to me that to those who have not used the toilet or gone to the bathroom for anything except a bath, the bathroom is a mystical place. So, show him how to do it. If you're a bit uncomfortable, then just do a "dry run," going through the motions. It will help, I promise. By demystifying that big bowl next to the tub, you can eliminate a lot of fear.

# wet
## or dry?

2-4 years

Does your child understand the difference between being wet and being dry? Ask him if his diaper is wet and then check to see if he's right. It is important for him to know the

difference before potty training starts. Disposable diapers do too good a job of keeping your child dry for him to notice wetness but cloth diapers are perfect for this, as is training underwear that has a little pad in the bottom (to prevent leaks) but doesn't keep your child dry!

# is your child ready?
## 2-4 years  **introducing the potty**

Look for evidence that your child knows what the potty is and what it's for. I used to bring my potty-training-age children into the bathroom all the time, just to show them around. "This is the potty," I would say. "Instead of going pee in your pants, one day you can go here." Then we would wash our hands together.

# is your child ready?
## more than one        2-4 years

Do you have more than one toilet in your house? Does your child know this? The reason I ask is because we have a bathroom upstairs and downstairs and after my last child was potty trained, I would find him coming downstairs at night to use the bathroom (the one he had been trained in). It occurred to me that he had never gone in the upstairs bathroom before, so I needed to let him know that he could use that bathroom as well. It was a bit of a surprise to him. Getting your child familiar with other bathrooms will also help him adjust to using the ones at school, in stores, and at other people's houses.

# is your child ready?

**2-4 years**

# the urge
# to go

Does your child let you know when she is about to wet or soil her diaper? This is an excellent indication that she is ready because it means she recognizes the urge to go. But don't freak out the first time she says this and start ripping her pants and diaper off. File it for future use and then tell her that when she feels like that, she can sit in this "beautiful new potty chair" you picked out together. If you've noticed that she does a little dance or something similar when she needs to go, bring the chair to her from time to time and see if she would like to try it out.

# can your child follow directions?

2-4 years

I know this sounds almost silly, but if your child can follow directions and also make the link between the "command" and the "action" needed, this is a good thing. Can your child find his jacket when you ask him and then know to put it on? Or maybe take his plate and carry it to the sink after dinner? Not many children will follow the commandment, "Pick up thine toys now," but if you ask him to help you with a chore, such as picking up a dirty pair of socks off the floor and bringing them to the laundry room, then you might have the makings of a "directions follower" on your hands. Give it some practice, then try it with the potty.

2-4 years

# hero undies

Encourage your child to think that underwear is fun to wear! Seeing a friend's cool new Superman undies, or daddy's boxers, can be a trigger for your child to want some of his own. Diapers are, after all, uncomfortable to some extent and very bulky, so it shouldn't be such a surprise that your child wants an alternative, and you should reinforce this. If your child is adamant that he wants "big boy" underwear, this is a sign of his growing interest in, well ... that area.

# is your child ready?
# no, no, no!

A "NO!" stage. Every child has them. A period (which feels like forever) when she says "no!" to everything. This is not a good time to start potty training! Even if your child exhibits other signs of readiness, work on the negativity first. Could there be added sources of stress in your lives. A new baby? A mom or dad who recently went back to work? Maybe it's something as simple as a schedule change or new activities. Maybe it's nothing at all and your child just likes to say "no" right now. Whatever it is, starting to train at this point will definitely be more frustrating for both of you. So, take a breath and keep reading those potty-training story books or even buy a potty, but don't try to force it, because it will only make everyone positively dismal about the whole idea.

# is your child ready?

**diaper discontent**

OK, don't get disgusted, but there are some children who simply like being in a dirty diaper. I know, I know, "ick!" But it's true. I once heard child-care expert Dr. Penelope Leach explain it to a mom this way: your child doesn't know what's so disgusting about it and it could just feel like a soft, squishy mud puddle! However, if your child is visibly displeased with what is in her diaper or even wakes up dry in the morning, then this is a sign she is ready to do it elsewhere. And it could happen overnight, so keep your eyes open for signs of diaper discontent.

# dressed for it

If your child is able to put on her pants or shirt, then she is certainly capable of toilet training. Even being able to do something as simple as getting her pants up and down is a good sign. But, we've got to make it easy for them. If your child is showing a genuine interest, then buy her some pants with an elastic waistband. Save those fancy button-fly jeans for when she's older! There is nothing more frustrating for a little one than to get all the way to the potty, and not be able to pull down her pants, or get them back on.

# parents ...
# are you ready?

Maybe your child seems ready, but are you? Potty training can be tough and you have to be willing to stick with it for as long as three months. If you don't have the time, and your child is only somewhat into it, don't even get started. Wait until you and other people in your child's life can help out. There is no sense in telling your child that the potty is the only place to "do it" if you are just going to throw a diaper on him every time you have to go out or "don't have time to deal with it." This only sends confusing messages and encourages your child to think that the potty is not really that important.

# be patient

2-4 years

It's an obvious tip, I know, but when you begin training, it seems so easy. You lovingly show your child the potty. You cheerfully read the books. But, after three weeks of reading the same book, cleaning up poopy underpants, and a house that smells of disinfectant, we are bound to lose our Mary Poppins quality. So, stay patient, try counting to ten, or remind yourself of the goal and how much better it will be once you get there.

## are you ready?

# take a month

I know, what am I crazy? And no, I don't mean taking a month off work if you are working. What I mean is to set aside a month during which you travel minimally and stick to an uncomplicated schedule. If your child goes to daycare, then continue to take him. If he has regular playdates or activities, then continue with them as well. But don't take that trip to Disneyworld during this period. Allow a month, making that first week the most intense, and really decide that this is when the potty training will happen. You will need to enlist everyone, from grandparents to babysitters, in this process as well. Let them know that you are serious—that your child is ready—and that you are making a concerted effort to make this work.

# choose when is best   2-4 years

Are you going through a life-changing event? New job? New schedule? New house? New baby? Then this is not the time to begin! If something is causing stress in your life, then most likely it is causing stress in your child's life as well. Adding potty training to the list won't help either one of you.

# are you ready?

**2-4 years**  **take a breather**

You don't seem to be getting anywhere. And sometimes you'll be thinking, "What could possibly be so hard about this? Just go in the potty!" But step back. If you are really having a hard time, maybe your child isn't ready. If your child is still proud of himself for using the potty, but doesn't make it all the time, then hang on. You're getting there. But be calm. If you lose it, you might have to start all over again.

# don't obsess

Something happens to parents when our child's second birthday comes around. All of a sudden it is very important that they get on the potty . . . and like it. Soon, our lives become totally obsessed with the bathroom and words like "pee pee" and "poopy." Calm down. Half the time, kids at two aren't the slightest bit interested. And why should they be? I know it's difficult. We all want signs and signals that we are good parents, and after baby starts to walk, talk, and eat on his own, the milestones become fewer and farther apart. But don't obsess about it or you'll be missing a lot of really golden opportunities with your child. I promise, he won't go to kindergarten in his diapers—and definitely not to college!

# messy starts

2-4 years

Your child has just said that she can go potty by herself. You are stunned and remind her to call you if she needs help. She comes out, proudly announcing that she is finished. You go to help her pull up her pants and then you check the toilet to make sure she flushed. Nothing in the toilet. You look up, you look down, then you slowly feel the

wetness in your slipper. Yup. She missed. Now, before you scream "Aagghhh!" remember, she made it to the bathroom and she got her pants down. There are going to be many messes ahead, and if you accept that right off the bat, you'll be way ahead of the game.

# don't be embarrassed 2-4 years

There is nothing more attention grabbing while you are having a quiet dinner in a nice restaurant than your two-and-a-half-year-old announcing he has "to poop now." OK, maybe a two-and-a-half-year-old who just peed on the restaurant's new carpet is more embarrassing. But the thing is, we parents have to accept the icky deeds, so there's no point scolding your toddler in a public bathroom while changing his pants. There is no call for embarrassment or scolding when, as Robin Williams put it, "the great poo poo" is involved. Just get over it, clean the kid up, and tell him "better luck next time." I have found, even in fancy restaurants, that most customers are more annoyed by a parent yelling or scolding their child, than by the actual act ... I know I certainly am.

# are you ready?

# define your terms

Be relaxed in your definition of potty training. It's happened to all of us. You go to the playgroup or the Tupperware party and there is undoubtedly one mother there who has a child who was potty-trained before the age of two. Well first, "yeah" for her. I often find that these mothers are the same ones who had babies who slept through the night from the day they got home from the hospital, but I digress. More often than not

I discover, after I have talked to the mother a little longer, that the miraculous toddler, who goes to the potty every two hours, has habituated mom into putting her on the potty at those intervals. In other words, if mom wasn't trained to put her on the potty, the child would go in her pants. See? It starts to become clearer. You have to define acceptable potty training for you and your child. Is day-trained more important than night-trained? Is there a difference? To some there is. Is your child potty-trained only if you stay in the house? So don't feel humbled by the talk at toddler group because different people have different definitions of training.

2-4 years **don't be afraid to stop**

If you thought your child was ready, but things seem to be getting worse each day, just stop. There is nothing to say that once you start, you can't stop. Absolutely, you should continue if there is any hope of progress, but if there isn't, cut your losses and take a break. The potty will be there in a month or two and while your child is getting older, you can reflect a bit on what went wrong, if anything. Whatever you do, don't give your child a guilt trip for stopping the training, because it will just make it worse later on.

My last child was absolutely enthralled with the potty, but after several days of great success, he would not get back on and

started to yell every time I wanted him to try. Apparently it was a fad he was trying out, and then he moved on to his new bicycle. So, I put the potty back in the bathroom, let him know that it was there, and told him to let me know if he wanted to use it. A few weeks later, he followed his older brother back into the bathroom and went potty again. Who knows? Sometimes, they just get it on their own timing.

are you ready?

## 2-4 years                    **be consistent**

I hate keeping quiet while I listen to a fellow parent complaining to me about how badly her child's potty training is going and yet every time I see the child, she's been put back in a diaper. If you're going to tell your child that this is it—it's the potty or nothing—then you have to be consistent. You can't cave in and use a diaper every time she has an accident. You can't put on a diaper when you go to the store because it will be easier. You have to commit and let your child know that you are serious and expect her to be serious too. But—and this is crucial—only if the child is as ready as you are.

## are you ready?
# the world of potty     2-4 years

Be ready to eat, sleep, and breathe potty talk. It seems like every time I potty trained a child, there was a three-month period when every other word had something to do with the potty. I was either cleaning it up, reading about it, buying supplies, or congratulating the child on a job well done. So, prepare yourself for the world of potty. It's time-consuming and often tedious, but the first time you walk down the baby aisle and don't have to buy diapers, it will all be worth it.

# getting started

She's ready and you're ready. Now what? Just how do you begin this seemingly monumental undertaking? Well, there's no mystical chant you must recite and no permit to apply for. It's just you and your child and that potty chair. Don't be intimidated, it's not rocket science, but at the same time, don't underestimate the difficulty of the task. Bringing home your baby was hard, but now she's a full-blown person with a lot of her own ideas about how to do things. So take a breath and if you're sure you're all ready, then just go ahead. But take a look at the following tips first to make sure you have everything you need to get started.

# picking the potty chair 2-4 years

There are lots of potty chairs to
choose from these days. Best
advice? Just pick a simple chair,
with a removable pot for easy
cleaning, with somewhere solid
to balance the feet (as pushing
down is critical for expelling),

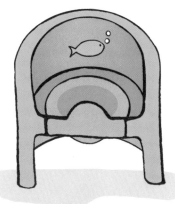

and perhaps with the ability to turn over into a footstool
for easy handwashing. Plastic potty seats that go over the
regular toilet are also handy, particularly when traveling, but
I have found that they make initial training difficult because
of the climbing involved and sometimes a child's innate fear
of the large toilet. After training four children, I have found
that the best way is to start from the ground up, as it were.

## getting started

2-4 years

# in the summertime

Start the potty-training process in the warm weather if at all possible. This is a great way to let your child feel her freedom and have less laundry at the same time. It's also easier when there are accidents because the child will undoubtedly be outside most of the time. We often let our little ones run around without anything on but a shirt during potty training and sometimes even brought the potty chair outside on the deck.

# avoid disposable training pants

2-4 years

They work just like diapers and your child will never feel just how wet he really is. Plain old underwear is the best because it gets soggy and cold and feels terrible. Your child knows right away he's peed in his pants and you get to be the hero who shows him how to avoid that situation.

# getting started

**multi purchase**

If you have a multi-level house, buy more than one potty chair. During my third child's training, the bathroom was upstairs. There was no way he could climb the stairs and make it in time. So, we bought a plastic potty chair that looked just like the one upstairs and placed it in a corner of his play area. It was out of the way for a little privacy, but right in the middle of things so he couldn't forget about it.

# have dad help

If you have boys, have dad show them how it's done. It sounds a little goofy, but more than one mother has told me that her little boy couldn't figure out why he had to stand until dad showed him how. It works too! One lesson and boys suddenly understand the power of aiming!

# hit the spot

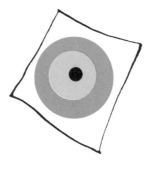

How about buying or making your own floating paper targets (they're sold online and in many baby departments) to help your son to sharpen his aim. One of my sons was so eager to sink the targets that were bobbing on the water that he forgot completely about diapers in a matter of days.

# potty practice

Let your child participate in the purchase of the potty and underpants, and when you bring them home, let her just have the potty around without being required to do anything in it. My fourth child frequently sat on my third child's potty fully clothed, reading a magazine. It was a riot, of course, and it made the transition a little easier because he was already familiar with the purpose of the strange little chair in the bathroom. In fact, I often found that he would pee in his diaper while he was sitting on the potty, indicating to me that he was getting ready.

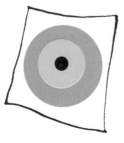

# getting started

## wipes forever

Keep those baby wipes around! I know, I know, you thought once the potty training began, the visits to the baby aisle would be over, but not quite. Baby wipes are indispensable (as all moms and dads know) for getting your little one's behind clean. They are also great to have around for use in public bathrooms.

# fear of poo!

I didn't believe it myself when I first read about it, but little kids can be afraid of almost anything, including flushing and watching their pee or poo go down the drain. My first child had a very real fear of his poop when he first saw it properly—he looked into the potty with a look of horror on his face, as if he couldn't believe what had come out of him. In retrospect, I realized he had never actually seen it before—it was always in the diaper that I quickly tossed away. Explain, in frank, simple terms, that the poop is normal, but it's a little yucky, and the toilet is taking it out—like taking out the trash. I always explained it as the stuff he ate that his body doesn't need (you keep the good stuff and the rest has to go down the drain). It may take a little while for your child to get the idea, but he will.

2-4 years **fear of the flush**

My fourth child hated the noise of the flush and to this day still covers his ears when he flushes in a public restroom (the echoing sound bugs him). The thing to do here, I have found, is to let the child flush the toilet a few times before he uses it—let him throw in a piece of toilet paper and watch with him as it goes down. As with a fear of poo, if you explain the system of the flush in simple and playful terms, the easier it will be for your child. Alternatively, flush the toilet for them until they are ready, and reassure your child that they cannot be sucked in and end up being flushed down the drain.

# water, water, water     2-4 years

The more she drinks, the more she'll have to pee! That doesn't mean buying gallons of bottled water and flushing (forgive the pun) your child's system completely. But giving water instead of dehydrating, sugary drinks (a good idea at any time), and easing up on binding foods like bananas and rice in favor of cereals or even goldfish crackers, will make the urge to eliminate come more regularly, making training a little easier.

# losing steam

You've read all of the books and watched all of the videos. Your child loves the idea of the potty and does the potty dance to let you know she has to go. Perhaps she has even gone on the potty consistently for a week or more. Then, nothing. She starts to have accidents. First, maybe just one or two—no big deal, you think. But then they become more frequent and suddenly, all talk of the potty has disappeared. It's almost like your child is saying, "been there, done that," and just wants to go back to her old life—where you did all the cleaning up. What do you do with a child who has lost all interest in the potty?

# draw a picture

For an older child, family therapist Dr. Gayle Peterson advocates drawing a simple diagram of the bladder, or holding a small balloon filled a quarter full with water and using your fingers to show how we can use our sphincter muscles to hold on and let go of urine at will. Ask her if she can tell when her bladder is "this full ...?" or "that full?" Make it clear that her body can learn this process now because she is old enough to use these muscles.

# is it painful?

Sometimes a child will refuse to go because they are constipated and going to the potty has become painful. Check and make sure your child's stools are soft and formed. Small, pebbly stools can indicate constipation, as can exceedingly large ones. Increase the amount of fiber in your child's diet if this seems to be the case (by introducing more wholegrain food and cereals). A urinary tract infection (which is more common in girls) may be to blame, causing pain or a burning sensation when your child tries to pee (*see pages 106–107* for more on illness). This could cause your child to hold off peeing for as long as possible until an accident becomes inevitable. Check with your doctor in both cases to see if there are other issues involved.

# have a toilet sit

2-4 years

Up to ten times a day, just take time out for your child to go and sit on the toilet. Make it a regular part of her day so that it becomes a habit. This way she knows that going to the toilet is just part of daily life and isn't interrupting all other activities. Often children stop wanting to go to the bathroom because it isn't novel or fun anymore. Toilet sits integrate the activity back into the normal flow of things.

losing steam

## gentle encouragement

2-4 years

Stay relaxed—I know it's hard! A child who faces a stern or even angry parent might refuse to go to the bathroom at all because he fears a negative outcome. Continual pushing can have the opposite effect on a once enthusiastic child, forcing him to push back—by going potty on the floor!

# making the connection

It could be that your child has not really connected the idea of sitting on the toilet with the idea of actually peeing in it yet. If you put your child on the potty several times when he was just about to go, the peeing part may have been secondary to the shock of having his pants taken off and being placed on a plastic chair with a hole in it. Getting your child to pee on the potty voluntarily (rather than you putting him there when you think he needs to go) will help him make the connection—"Oh, I sit on this chair when I feel the urge to go, and then I go"—rather than, "Mommy sat me on this thing and pee came out."

# losing steam

# use some rules

If your child just doesn't have time for that potty thing because there is a sandbox full of friends waiting for him outside, then make some rules. A famous line in my house is, "Does anyone have to go to the bathroom?" before we leave for anywhere or before the kids go out to play in the backyard. This cuts down on accidents for the little ones and, in the case of the ten-year-old, limits my trips to public bathrooms!

## potty books

*losing steam*

2-4 years

Sometimes a child just needs a reason to go to the bathroom, besides the urge to pee (remember, it doesn't always bother your child as much as it does you when she goes in her pants!). Take your child to the local bookstore and pick out two or three picture books that she just loves. Maybe they're the kind with the noisy buttons that you have refused to buy up until now. What's the catch? She can only read them while she is going to the potty. For a couple of days, you might find her in there all the time (that's a good thing), and hopefully, going to the potty will become a comfortable experience. At least it won't be as boring as looking at the wallpaper for ten minutes.

2-4 years

# potty pops

There is a trademarked brand of "Potty Pops" on the market, but parents can make their own pops by using diluted fruit juice in popsicle molds. Do not give potty pops at any other time or for any other reason except after successfully using the toilet. Give them consistently after each use for three to six weeks. After this initial training period, give potty pops only when your child remembers and requests one. Eventually, toilet training will become a learned, conditioned reflex, and potty pops will not be necessary for reinforcement.

# put your child in charge

2-4 years

If your child feels like the only thing she is doing is peeing—and maybe just because you told her to—then she might be feeling a bit left out. Let her empty the pot into the toilet, rinse it out and put it back in place. In addition, if your child "missed," let her help clean it up (at least the edge of the mess!). This will particularly reinforce the importance of going in the potty, since she probably will join you in making a couple of "ick" sounds while wiping up.

2-4 years **throw out
the disposables**

If your child is really ready and you get the feeling she is just dawdling, throw out all the alternatives. Don't make a huge deal about it, but if she is old enough to come up to you and ask for a diaper, then she is old enough to understand when you tell her there aren't any left. But don't leave yourself an opening by saying, "The store ran out," because a smart three-year-old will tell you to go to another store! Just tell her that diapers and disposable training pants don't belong in a house with a big girl like her who can use the potty.

losing steam

# did you lose interest?

2-4 years

Sometimes it's not so much the child who loses interest as the parents. I realized my son began to lose interest in going potty when I started to act like it was normal for him to go. My lack of enthusiasm for his potty training was affecting his desire to carry on. Some kids, like my son, still need a few cheers even a month or two after they have successfully potty trained. So keep your enthusiasm and excitement levels high, and hopefully your child will, too.

# to bribe or not
# to bribe?

In every book I read or Internet discussion I peek in on, this seems to be one of the most hotly debated areas of potty training. Do we bribe our children to use the potty? There are excellent arguments both for and against, but it comes down to your basic parenting philosophy. Consider it this way: are you the kind of parent who will pay your child for chores as she gets older? Or will you expect a certain amount of contribution from your child to the general household and perhaps give an allowance? The following tips illustrate some of the benefits and pitfalls of "reward systems." The most important thing is to choose a method that you feel comfortable with, without letting your child—or another parent—tell you which way is best.

# stickers system

2-4 years

One mom used this method. Label a piece of paper with a goal or reward (like going to her favorite park, ice skating, the zoo, and so on). Then, every time your child uses the potty, she gets a sticker to put on the paper. When the page is filled with stickers, give the child the reward listed on the paper. Remember to keep the rewards tangible and easily achieved, especially at the beginning (for example, requiring ten stickers for a small prize may be too much for some children).

# to bribe or not to bribe?

## candy

Many parents use candy as a reward, and a few small treats after a successful potty trip seems to be the most popular. I will freely admit to bribing my firstborn with yogurt-covered raisins when he was first training, and they worked (one for pee, two for poop—a common equation, I have discovered). Just be careful not to overload the child, and watch for signs that he is expecting or demanding his reward. Again, make some rules. One good rule is that candy is only given for something actually produced in the potty, not just for sitting on it.

# to bribe or not to bribe?

# the argument against  2-4 years

Some experts say that for the sake of your child's dental care and dietary habits, candy is the worst reward. Not only is it bad for their teeth, but it may also interfere with their appetite for meals; and it is not uncommon to find a child peeing a drop of urine every five minutes just to get that candy treat. I say use your own discretion on this one. Candy or even yogurt-covered raisins can be a powerful motivator, and if it's working, then don't mess with success.

# to bribe or not to bribe?

## 2-4 years potty peer pressure

Does your child go to day care, or can she spend some time with other children who are potty training at least part of the day? This is a great bribe in itself. Children who are around other children who use the potty are more inclined to want to use it themselves. It's the exact opposite of what we want children to do in most every other situation, but in potty training, peer pressure can actually be a benefit! Just make sure she isn't being teased for still using diapers.

# cheerleading

2–4 years

Keep a check on your child's pants and let her know how great it is that she is staying dry. This, combined with huge praise when your child uses the potty, is often reward enough. When my youngest started potty training, the whole family got in on the act. Big brothers and big sister would do a little parade when he emerged from a successful potty run and we would all clap and shout for him. The hero's welcome he received every time he came out of the bathroom was better than any handful of candy.

2-4 years

# real underwear

Getting to dress just like mom, dad, or brothers and sisters is another great reward in itself. This was particularly motivating for my younger sons who went shopping with me for underwear for my older children. I distinctly remember my youngest pitching the package of diapers out of the cart and grabbing for a package of underwear, like his big brother's.

He wasn't quite ready yet, but the message was clear. I bought him some regular underwear and after several successful attempts at using the potty, he was allowed to wear them. He also felt bad when he soiled them. I swear, I didn't say anything derogatory at all, but I was pleased with the effect his guilt had on his training process!

# to bribe or not to bribe?

2-4 years **let everybody know**

It is important that everyone in your child's life—caregivers, grandparents, friends—understands the plan of attack. Get them in on the act. My mother used to call and tell one of her grandchildren that she heard they were using the potty and would even tell them funny stories about my sisters and me when we were first learning. It made them feel extra special and also alleviated a bit of the stress, knowing they had the goods on mom!

# to bribe or not to bribe?

2-4 years

# throw a party

Invite her friends and relatives. Have a little celebration for a month of dry pants ... or however long you feel is right. You can take this idea as far as you like—a potty theme could be created with appropriate favors and even a potty-shaped cake, or you could just have a little lunch. Either way, your child will feel special, and if you invite kids who are not yet trained, it could inspire them to drier days as well! Top it off with a ceremonial throwing out (or giving away, if someone you know could use them) of what's left of the diapers.

2-4 years **know when to end it**

When mastery is achieved, it's time to stop the rewards. Frequently kids lose interest as toilet use becomes second nature and you may have no trouble. Others may hang on to the idea and continue to demand rewards for each successful potty trip. If this is the case, keep the praise high and perhaps redirect your rewards system into a chores list. He'll still get a reward now and then, but it will be for things like picking up toys or wiping down the dinner table.

# promises, promises

2-4 years

Daphne Metland, the former editor of *Parent's Magazine* and a featured expert at *Babycentre.co.uk*, says that asking your child to promise to use the potty doesn't work well. Saying, "If we stop at the toy store on the way home to get you that game, you have to promise to use the toilet all afternoon," or "If I let you wear your party dress without a diaper, promise me you won't have any accidents," probably won't do much good. It's useless to ask young children to stick to a promise in the future in exchange for something they want at that moment. So instead, offer attainable treats after they have managed to go potty.

# to bribe or not to bribe?

## 2-4 years

# pants on fire

Most experts agree that punishing your child at any time for acts related to the potty is not necessary. Just because a child promised to stay dry, and then didn't, does not mean they "lied" to you (if I hadn't heard one parent say it, I wouldn't be saying it here in this book!). Most children are very intelligent and can quickly figure out when they will get praise and rewards and how to make that happen more often. The important thing is to be patient (as always), recognize a little deceptiveness when it is happening, and act accordingly, remaining positive and cheerful throughout the training period. One mother learned to distinguish between actual pee in the potty and the water her child had put in so she could get an extra treat. She started giving her daughter "pretend" treats for each time water was used. The daughter, of course, complained: "That's not a real treat." The mother replied, "When you put in real pee, I'll give you a real treat." Keep your sense of humor—you'll get your revenge when you tell that story to your daughter's fiancé!

# training
## and traveling

It's a phrase we used to hear frequently in my car and one of the most dreaded: "I've gotta go potty—right now!" The first thing I can tell you right off the bat about traveling with a potty-training toddler is that, if you aren't already, you will become a connoisseur of public bathrooms. You will know, without hesitation, the location of every option for a potty break within a one-hour radius of your house. Soon, you will not remember certain restaurants for their cuisine, but because they once allowed you to use the bathroom without requiring a purchase. There are many ways to make traveling with your potty trainee easier, but the most important of them all is, as always, to have a sense of humor about the whole scenario.

# home's best

If your child is making good progress at home but is unable just yet to comprehend the idea of going in an unfamiliar place, try postponing (if you can) that long trip. Some kids are frightened by public toilets. I couldn't have paid my firstborn with a truckload of candy to go to the porta-potty during one road trip and, of course, it made for a wet ride.

2-4 years

# take along the potty chair

An unfamiliar and potentially scary public toilet becomes immediately recognizable when the potty seat from home is put on top. If you don't want to travel with the potty chair, purchase a toilet seat adapter ring. Just remember to ignore the teenage girls staring at you as they fill up their car while you drag your squirming toddler, and the very conspicuous potty ring, into the bathroom. Someday, they'll know what it's all about!

# just for boys

I have three boys and this tip was perfect for them, although it is completely useless for girls. If you are really in a jam, meaning there's not a toilet to be found for miles and you're on a busy highway so you don't want the child to pee on the side of the road (or if dad is trying to make time and is sick of stopping every 30 minutes!), use a jar or a bottle. I know, it sounds gross, but as a family that does a lot of back-roads trawling, it was—and still is—immensely useful. Just offer the jar and let your child let loose. Make sure it has a lid! Wrap it up in a plastic bag and keep it steady until you can dispose of it.

training and traveling

2-4 years                    # get over it

It's going to happen. Sometimes you just can't hold it in any longer. Try to get comfortable with the idea of letting a child, particularly a boy, pee on the side of the road. No one is going to be upset if they see a three-year-old letting loose into the grass. Some kids, especially well-potty-trained ones, think it's wrong to go outside, so reassure your child that it's fine (only when in a jam). But be warned—I knew a toddler who, much to my horror, started whipping his pants down at the beach!

# quick change artist     2-4 years

Keep a spare change of clothes within reach. I know, I know, you have a bunch in the suitcase, but the suitcase is either buried under two days' worth of granola bars and juice boxes or is on top of the car. Keep a plastic grocery or large Ziplock bag under your seat, ready for a quick change—the bag is perfect for storing the wet clothes when done.

# going to a hotel?

Pack a plastic tablecloth or rubber sheet to put under his sheets in bed. It may be that your child has never wet the bed and is perfectly potty-trained, but being away from home can wreak havoc with even the most seasoned pro. Ever have that feeling of waking up in a hotel room and not remembering quite where you are? Well, imagine that and not knowing where or even if there is a bathroom. You can also get cotton mattress protectors that go over the bed sheet. These are easily removed and great in hotels where you can't change the sheets yourself. Besides, the sheet works great under the car seat as a protector against juice spills and cracker crumbs!

# travel potties

2-4 years

If you are taking the potty along, line it with a disposable plastic bag. This makes that walk to the garbage can much easier for dad (and I always made dad do it!) and avoids the need to clean and disinfect the bowl.

Traveling potties are also great at the beach, if there is only one adult, or at fairs and the like. No lines and none of that smell! If you can't find a private place for your child to use the travel potty, block her with the stroller or make a pretend wall with a beach towel.

79

# flying?

Susan Burke, a writer for *keepingkidshealthy.com*, had this to say about flying and potty training: "Potty training and air travel pose a particular challenge. Since both toddlers and flights are unpredictable, it is not always possible to make that emergency trip to the bathroom when your child has to go 'right now.' We learned this the hard way when we ended up with a soaking wet seat halfway through a five-hour flight. If you are in the process of potty training, forget it during your flight. Put your toddler in pull-ups or diapers for the entire trip. Also, be sure to carry with you a complete change of clothes,

because accidents happen." So I guess the message here is that flying is an exception. Most parents find the flight is a trial without worrying about potty training, so if your kid has an accident on a plane, let it go, or, in this circumstance, break the rules and use a diaper to avoid problems.

# wipes out

Have baby wipes installed in your car if possible. Just kidding, but only partly. Baby wipes are the other indispensable part of potty training while on the road. They can be useful for everything from wiping a bottom after a successful potty trip to handwashing afterward. Let's face it, some of those public bathrooms are just disgusting and I would rather clean my child up next to my own van, than stand in a porta-potty for even a minute more!

## training and traveling
# going backward
### 2-4 years

Pediatrician Dr. William Sears says that, "Sometimes toilet training is easier while on vacation. You have more time and patience, baby is often a bare-bottomed beach bum, and you are not so concerned about messes. However, some children relapse while on vacation. If this happens, delay until you return home. Also remember that a change in diet during family vacations is likely to bring about a change in bowel habits, either constipation or diarrhea, and a corresponding slump in training progress."

# public restrooms

Before your child begins to potty train, and certainly during, bring her into the bathroom with you at a variety of places. Get her used to the idea that it is all right to sit on this other potty and then wash hands afterward. Expose her to a variety of toilets. This was a lesson learned when I discovered, in a rest area in New York, that my youngest was terrified of toilets that flush on their own after the user gets up. If you're the kind of person who finds the use of toilet seat covers on public toilets necessary, then demonstrate how to use them and what they're for. This will make her first foray into that bright public bathroom a more comfortable one!

# keeping your
# child clean

One of the biggest challenges for both parent and child alike during the weeks of potty training—and the years after—is maintaining good hygiene practices. It may seem like a no-brainer, but even once your child is completely trained, you will still have to remind her about washing hands and wiping correctly. Whoever said that having a potty-trained child was easier than one still in diapers was dead wrong. Sometimes I think even more work is involved because you constantly have to check their progress and continue to clean up after them. Good hygiene practices are also necessary as your child goes off to daycare or school because more than one disease has been spread due to unwashed hands!

## express clean

2-5 years

When accidents happen—and they will happen—change your child as quickly as possible. Without the protection of a diaper, urine or stools can become irritating and you could encounter diaper rash all over again, especially if the child "dries off" before the change is made. Make sure to clean your child thoroughly after an accident, including the legs, since the diaper is no longer there to contain the mess.

A shower with a detachable spray nozzle is ideal, as a bath allows the child to sit in water with her own mess.

# Keeping clean

## just for girls

Proper wiping is essential and special attention must be paid to girls. First, keep baby wipes on hand to wipe after a bowel movement, since they are much easier to use and clean a child quicker than regular toilet paper. Some brands are flushable, which eliminates an accidental overflow in the bathroom garbage pail. Girls need to learn to wipe front to back in order to prevent contamination from the rectum. Also, teach girls to pat the front area as opposed to wiping hard, which can cause irritation and rashes.

# gentleman, wipe the seat

My piano teacher had a funny little saying framed in her bathroom. It said: "If you sprinkle when you tinkle, please be neat and wipe the seat." Boys, especially younger ones, are notorious for not putting the seat up (or back down) when they pee, but also for missing and getting it on the seat (and behind it and on the floor). Teach your child to wipe the seat with toilet paper when he's done (and before he washes his hands!) because germs can be spread this way and because it's considerate to the next person.

# Keeping clean

**now wash your hands**

I spent some time working in a hospital as a nursing assistant and if there is anything I learned, and retained, it is the method for proper handwashing. I was amazed at just how poorly I had been doing it. I have since passed on to my children the importance of washing to the wrists and between fingers. I have also taught them that, even though it uses a bit more water, if they are in a public restroom, it is important to get a paper towel and dry their hands before turning off the water. Then, use the paper towel to shut off the water. I had never thought about it before, but everyone comes out of the bathroom and turns on the water tap, meaning that turning it off with your freshly washed hand becomes virtually useless if you re-touch the faucet handle.

# keep disinfectant handy 2-5 years

Repeated uses and misses in a potty chair mean a lot of cleaning up will be required. The best cheap and easy disinfectant is a simple solution of bleach and water in a spray bottle. Although commercial brands are available, I have found this, coupled with rolls of paper towels at the ready, is the most cost-effective solution. Two capfuls of bleach in a filled water bottle is more than enough to keep the germs away, but make sure you keep the spray bottle out of reach from your kids.

# follow up

Expect to continue to follow your child into the bathroom long after he is trained. This was one of the things I found hardest to realize. I just thought, "Oh, he's trained, I don't have to do this any more." Wrong! I am forever reminding and still, until the age of probably four or five depending on the child, supervising and occasionally finishing up the job of wiping a butt. Boys seem to learn the wiping lesson later than girls because, quite frankly, girls have to wipe every time, but boys can just leave when they're done. Keep a check on them and remind even the child who is closing the door and demanding privacy to wipe. If they don't, you'll know about it in that next load of laundry.

# paper round 2-5 years

There is nothing more infuriating than a toilet full of paper and a disgusting mess all over the floor. It is essential to show children the appropriate amount of toilet paper to use. Whether you are a folder or wadder, you only need so much going down the drain. Also make sure your child understands that toilet paper is the only kind of paper that goes down the toilet. I have had to remove paper towels, newspaper, and even a picture someone obviously didn't like!

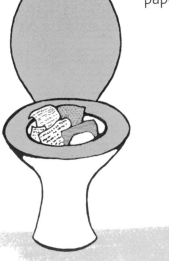

# toilet seat lining

If you are very worried about germs and are in the habit of using paper toilet liners when in a public restroom, then make sure your child understands how to use them as well. If paper liners are not available in the restroom, then show your child how to line the toilet with strips of toilet paper. On the other hand, don't be surprised if your child frequently omits this step. Sometimes just getting to the potty on time is a heroic action in itself and good hand washing and wiping should be enough to prevent even the most stubborn of germs.

# going swimming? 2-5 years

It is imperative that you are confident in your child's potty training before you let her go without a diaper in a swimming pool. *E. coli* and other nasty diseases can spread easily to other swimmers when a child lets

loose in the warm, comfortable environment of the pool. Using a diaper? Then be sure to buy a special swimmer's diaper (there are many kinds available) that will prevent leaks because many regular diapers fill up to an immense size when underwater and frequently burst!

# throw it out

Get rid of overly soiled underwear. Sometimes you just can't save it and frankly, there were times when my little one exploded and I was all too pleased just to ditch the underwear. Urine-soaked undies are easily washed in hot water and a little bleach and will come out smelling like new. Even a pair of underwear with an easily tossed (into the toilet) stool will be able to be reused with a hot water wash, but anything, let's say, "wetter" than that should just go.

# keep the toilet clean 2-5 years

I'm sure you do this already, but remember: little ones are explorers and they will play with the toilet. You want them to be comfortable around the toilet, after all. But they will lift the lid, run their cars around it, and all kinds of other fun stuff. Use a toilet lock if you are worried about drowning potential or objects being stuffed down the toilet. However, we want our children to be as familiar with the toilet as the potty chair, and so both need to be disinfected. Some companies sell ready-to-go flushable disinfectant wipes (they're just like baby wipes with bleach) to make the process quick. Just don't confuse them with your child's wipes!

# accidents will happen

Your child will have been going on the potty successfully for days, weeks even, and then one day, she'll just forget, and the mess will begin again. Every child has accidents. Even children who seem to have been trained forever will, at some point, have too much excitement one day or just be plain sick of going to the potty. As always, patience is the key to dealing with accidents, because showing more than mild disappointment may cause a power struggle between you and your child, with her revenge being the mess in her pants.

accidents

# is your child too young? 2-5 years

If your child is too young, accidents may be more likely
to happen. Children under two years of age
are generally not considered capable of
controlling the sphincter muscles. They
may potty train temporarily in a fit of
excitement and wonder at the idea,
particularly if a reward system is in place
to encourage the training. If your child is
very young (some mothers report potty-
trained children as young as 16 months),
keep the potty around, but back off the
hard-core training. The child is probably
not able to understand fully exactly
what she is doing, but knows enough
to enjoy the praise for it.

# clean up kid

Get your child to help you clean up after the accident. Whether he puts the clothes in the washer or helps you clean up the floor, he will see that accidents have consequences beyond the wet pants. This isn't a punishment, just a way to keep your child in the mix. If he thinks that everything magically becomes clean after the accident, he won't have an incentive to stop. I use this same method with spilled juice in the living room (that's why mommy tells you to drink it in the kitchen) and other messes.

# accidents
# don't despair     2–5 years

If accidents are infrequent, keep the obvious disappointment down to a minimum. It is so easy to sigh heavily or get angry when your child wets his pants again. But take a second, count to ten, and gently remind your child about using the potty. Don't be afraid of showing some disappointment, since most children want to please and it is not harmful to use that (gently, of course) to our advantage. Just make sure that every time your child does use the potty, he gets warm praise and a round of applause.

**changes**

Even if you trained your child during a stress-free period

of your life, any new stressors are bound to create a little

reaction in a preschooler, and this often happens in his

pants. A new baby brother or sister, a change in a parent's

work schedule, a new house, or a new school (even a new daycare teacher) can provoke worry or cause your child to want to lash out by having an accident. Try to ease the stress by spending time with your child at the end of the day, talking about new things, reading stories that treat the issue at hand, or even role-playing the new parts of the day. Always add a, "Need to stop by the potty?" and make sure your child knows that you're not angry with them for their transgressions. Most experts say that as the child readjusts to the routine, and with continuing encouragement from a parent, the child should stop having accidents on their own. On the other hand, some children have accidents to get your attention. Don't be afraid to make your displeasure known, but give the child ample opportunity to please you in other ways, like helping with chores.

# accidents

## potty breaks

During daytime hours, many children have accidents because they don't want to stop what they are doing. It is important to remind them during play to take a potty break. First off, don't ask them if they want or have to go. Tell them, firmly, that it's time to go potty, such as: "After you go to the potty, we will go to the playground." This is especially important if you just watched your child down two juice boxes and then swears he doesn't have to go. Also, make sure that you enforce the rules (*see page 52*) about nobody leaving the house (even just to play in the backyard) without going potty first.

# set a timer

Sometimes, quite frankly, I just plain forget to ask my child if he has to go. I might be involved in something and he is probably playing intently and it just doesn't occur to me. It can be helpful to set a timer that will remind both of you that it's been a while.

# physical problems

A child who has frequent accidents could also have a physical problem, such as a urinary tract infection. The National Institute of Health says that, "If your child is an infant or is only a few years old, the signs of a urinary tract infection may not be clear, since children that young cannot tell you just how they

feel. Your child may have a high fever, be irritable, or not eat. On the other hand, sometimes a child may have only a low-grade fever, experience nausea and vomiting, or just not seem healthy. The diaper urine may have an unusual smell. If your child has a high temperature and appears sick for more than a day without signs of a runny nose or other obvious cause for discomfort, he or she may need to be checked for a bladder infection."

# everybody go!

Sometimes my little ones don't want to go to the bathroom because no one else has to. Even my frequent reminders won't work if the older children (who probably really don't have to go) say, "No, I don't have to" every time I ask. Getting my older children to go to the bathroom first (even if they just flush and wash their hands) goes a long way toward making a little one feel included. Sometimes, if the older kids aren't around, I'll go first (this also works if you have an only child). Don't

discount the idea that your child aspires to being a big kid—the big kids aren't constantly being reminded to use the bathroom and sometimes little ones feel out of place because they are.

# accidents
## during illness . . .
2–5 years

There will come a time when your newly potty-trained
child will have an illness or a bout of diarrhea that will make
accidents almost inevitable. The first thing to do is to remind
yourself that she is ill and that cleaning up such accidents
is a part of that. The second thing is to let your child know
that you understand that during an illness, this kind of thing
will happen. Go ahead and use a "big kid" training pant for
these situations. Just make sure your child understands that
this is only while she is sick. Most likely the child will feel
embarrassed or guilty about illness-related accidents so it's
important to continue to encourage her during this time,
but also not to show disapproval at the accident.

# keep a potty journal  2–5 years

Get a notebook and fill
it with the dates and
times of all potty-
related activities,
including accidents. You
might notice a trend in
your child's accidents if

they are rather frequent. Keeping the journal will help you

to figure out if he always has an accident after a certain

type of food or drink (indicating stomach upset?) or at a

certain time of day (perhaps indicating fatigue or worry over

an upcoming event, like going to a certain friend's house or

school). You can also let him participate in the journal by

drawing potty-related pictures, or happy faces or stars when

he succeeds in staying dry all day.

# accidents

2-5 years      **liquid levels**

This one may sound simple, but it has come up many times in my conversations with parents: restrict juice and milk intake. Not to levels that would be nutritionally deficient,

 but think about your preschooler. Does he have access to the refrigerator? Does he pour his own juice or milk, or do you have boxes so he doesn't have to? Does he not ask before he grabs something

to drink? If you answered "yes" to any of these then your child could be taking in too much sugar with his liquid, increasing dehydration and his need for more fluid, and therefore increasing his need to urinate and making accidents more likely. What do you do? Offer water. Keep a small cup available at all times for your child, next to the tap or your drinking water source. When a child is truly thirsty, he will drink water—when he just wants something sweet, he'll reach for the juice box.

# bedwetting

Most children wet the bed at some time or another. It could be an occasional thing, or it could happen nightly. The medical term for bedwetting is enuresis and it can be both stressful and embarrassing for parent and child alike. In America alone, between five and seven million children wet their beds, so it's nothing abnormal. Parents sometimes think their children are too lazy to get out of bed at night, but this is rarely the case. Bedwetting has nothing to do with how you potty trained your child and you should definitely not feel guilty. At the same time, children need to know that they are not at fault either and that, just like anything else, with a little practice and patience, it will eventually stop.

# what goes in . . .

Cut down on the three "C's"—carbonated drinks, chocolate, and caffeine, all of which can make bedwetting more likely. This does not mean eliminate all drinks (or chocolate for that matter). Your child should be encouraged to drink water before bed or anytime she is thirsty, and sodas and chocolate can occasionally be enjoyed after dinner as long as there is ample time to use the bathroom before bed.

# bedwetting

3-7 years     **too sleepy?**

Some children are very deep sleepers and just have trouble waking up in the middle of the night. Your child may often have water- or bathroom-related dreams, but not recognize what her body is telling her. One mother said her daughter told her, quite emphatically, that she had already gone to the bathroom. The little girl was absolutely convinced and her mother concluded that perhaps, just as grown-ups often imagine they are shutting off the alarm in the morning, her little girl dreamed the whole scenario. If your child sleeps very deeply, it could be worthwhile waking her up routinely during the night and taking her to the bathroom. This works for some parents who report that their child just needed to get in the habit of going in the middle of the night. Also, leave a nightlight on to guide your child to the bathroom.

# wake up call

A "moisture alarm" is an alternative to a parental wake up call. This is a small alarm that the child can wear when he goes to bed at night. When the child begins to wet the bed, the alarm goes off. After a while, the child may wake up on his own without the alarm, or he may learn to sleep all the way through the night without going to the bathroom. Some parents report success in as few as three months.

## bedwetting

**worried and wet**

Sometimes children who never wet the bed, or who haven't wet the bed for a long time, do so because they are worried or upset. The same stressors that can affect potty training can also affect a toddler: a new baby, a divorce, even a problem at school. So don't make a big deal out of the bedwetting. Recognize it as a symptom of a larger problem. As you and the child work through the stressor, the bedwetting should stop.

# pee date

bedwetting

3-7 years

More than a few parents say that getting their child up for one last pee before they turn in is a great way to keep kids dry. If your child is in bed at say, 8 P.M., and you go to bed at 11 P.M., make a pit stop before you turn in and take your child into the bathroom. Yes, this does disrupt their sleep slightly, but because most children are such deep sleepers they generally wake up only partially and will settle down again quickly. One mom said that after a short time, her daughter began to get up on her own and would "meet" her in the bathroom for the nightly pee.

## bedwetting

### 3–7 years

# don't stop having fun

Even kids who wet the bed should be allowed to go on sleepovers or to camp. If it's a huge problem, talk to the camp counselor or the parent about it. Most children who wet the bed at home don't wet the bed elsewhere because they don't sleep as deeply and might be self-conscious about the bedwetting. To make your child feel safer, purchase some "pull-up" type disposable underwear for nighttime use or one of the specially made sleeping bags with a sponge-type liner that will prevent the bag from getting wet (and being obvious!).

# alarm bells

Using an ordinary alarm clock can also be helpful. The idea is to have your child "beat the clock," and recognize the urge to urinate before the alarm goes off. The alarm should be

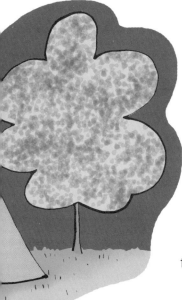

set for about three or four hours after bedtime. Place a nightlight or a flashlight at your child's bedside to illuminate the way to the bathroom. The alarm should be used nightly until your child can go three or four weeks without wetting the bed. This may also take three or four months.

## bedwetting

# quick clean-up

To make clean-up easier, every night before bed put clean pajamas on the dresser, at the ready, and place a towel or a rubber sheet beneath the sheet, but over the mattress. If you can find them at your local medical supplies store, those disposable mattress guards (they're about two feet wide and four feet long—probably last seen in the maternity ward when mom was giving birth) are perfect. They protect the mattress and clean up quickly. Have your child help with a quick clean-up. This is not a punishment, but a way for your child to help feel in control and get over the embarrassment of the situation.

# just like mom or dad

bedwetting 3–7 years

More than 77 percent of all children who wet the bed had bedwetting parents. Don't be shy about this. If you had troubles as a child, share them: your child is much more likely to feel less embarrassed and more optimistic. If you don't have personal experience of wetting the bed, maybe there is a relative or close friend who does and who would be willing to talk to your child—over an ice cream sundae—about it.

bedwetting

**honey trap**

Folk medicine pioneer Dr. D.C. Jarvis stood by honey as a
remedy for bedwetting. He said that a teaspoonful of honey
before bed can be helpful in two ways: as a mild sedative
for the nervous system, and as a fluid reducer during the
hours of sleeping. The levulose in the honey, he said, has a
moisture-absorbing ability (observable in baked goods) and
will hold the fluid, sparing the kidneys. In addition, the
honey method allows parents the opportunity to observe
whether certain conditions make bedwetting more likely—
a party or other excitement, for example. On "safe" nights,
you can reduce the amount of honey, or leave it out
altogether as the child begins to stay dry at night.

# medical advice

Discuss severe or perpetual bedwetting with your child's doctor. There could be physical issues (*see pages 106–107 on urinary tract infections*) that may be inhibiting your child's ability to control his bladder at night. In severe cases, there are some medications that could help your child stay dry at night, but some doctors warn that the success rate of such medications is not known, since children who take them may also be growing out of the bedwetting habit.

# further reading

BORGARDT, MARIANNE.
*What do You do with a Potty?
An Important Pop-up Book.*
Golden Books, 1994.

CAPUCILLI, ALYSSA SATIN.
*The Potty Book for Girls and
The Potty Book for Boys.*
Barron's Educational Series, Inc., 2000.

FRANKEL, ALONA.
*Once Upon a Potty—Girl and Boy
Book and Tape.*
HarperCollins Publishers, 1999.

KRUEGER, ANNE.
*Parenting Guide to Toilet Training.*
Ballantine Books, Inc., 2001.

TIPPINS, SHERILL (ED.).
*The American Academy of Pediatrics
Guide to Toilet Training.*
Bantam Books, Inc., 2003.

WAGNER, KATHI.
*Rugrats' Potty Book: A Baby's
Got to Go!*
Simon & Schuster Children's, 1998.

# notes

---

---

---

---

---

---

---

---

---

---

---

---

---

---

## Acknowledgments

I would like to thank my children, my husband, John Hogan, my mother, Rebecca Saraceno and Mandy Greenfield for all of their help and encouragement.

# index